LANDSCAPE WITH QUESTION

Leeanne Quinn's debut collection of poetry, *Before You* (Dedalus Press, 2012), was highly commended in the Forward Prize for Poetry 2013. Her second collection, *Some Lives* (Dedalus Press, 2020), was noted as a Book of the Year by *The Irish Times* and *The Irish Independent.* She co-edited *Romance Options: Love Poems for Today* (Dedalus Press, 2022) and is the editor of *Beginnings Over and Over: Four New Poets from Ireland* (Dedalus Press, 2025). Her poems have been widely anthologised, appearing in *The Forward Book of Poetry 2013*, *Windharp: Poems of Ireland Since 1916*, *Hold Open the Door: A Commemorative Anthology from The Ireland Chair of Poetry*, and *Queering The Green: Post-2000 Queer Irish Poetry*. She holds a PhD in American Literature from Trinity College Dublin. Originally from Drogheda and Monasterboice, Co. Louth, she has lived in Germany, Austria, and is now based in Limerick, Ireland.

LANDSCAPE WITH QUESTION

LEEANNE QUINN

CARCANET POETRY

First published in Great Britain in 2026 by
Carcanet
Main Library, The University of Manchester
Oxford Road, Manchester, M13 9PP
www.carcanet.co.uk

A CIP catalogue record for this book is
available from the British Library.

ISBN 978 1 80017 561 7

Book design by Andrew Latimer, Carcanet
Typesetting by LiteBook Prepress Services
Printed in Great Britain by SRP Ltd, Exeter, Devon

FSC www.fsc.org
MIX
Paper | Supporting responsible forestry
FSC® C014540

The publisher acknowledges financial
assistance from Arts Council England.

Supported using public funding by
ARTS COUNCIL ENGLAND

for Georgina

CONTENTS

I

II

III

Place. In a place,
A place for everything and everything in its place.
In place in place of everything, in a place.

– Gertrude Stein, 'An Elucidation',
transition (April 1927)

But I had to think long and hard about the Time, since 'today' is an impossible word for me, even though I hear and say it daily, you can't escape it.

– Ingeborg Bachmann, *Malina*,
tr. Philip Boehm

Then I went down there and suddenly began to see things.

– Nano Reid, *The Irish Times*,
6 July 1973

I

TRIPTYCH OF BIRTH YEARS FOR THE ARTIST NANO REID: 1900

Reasons for spring reasons for summer
reasons for autumn reasons for winter
the yard cat reasons itself into the sun
this first March of the new century

LANDSCAPE WITH DAFFODILS

Since I survived the winter, since I was so happy,
and it was already March, the first warm day
of the year. The ice rink had finally closed
and in the park the magnolias had begun to bloom.
I wanted to find the broad arrows, to know
the highest point. I was born 140ft above sea.
Where was I now? Where was the bed of daffodils
that turned into yellow-topped bins? I still remember
their apparent colour. Where were they now?
You could see a lot from the hill, and it was quite
beautiful. In winter I had to try harder —
think of the leaf, of the Stadtpark, of the daffodils
real in the distance, of the cars slowing down
at the gates of the park, of your hand
on the broad arrow. It must have been there
all along, but how much of my life
am I supposed to remember?

WATER IN SHADOW

I took the narrow road by the sea, past the ghost house
and the spot where the boy was drowned.

I remembered how the road veered before it veered.
If I only saw the bend while taking it
it would be too late.

The radio knew the time of day but I never switched it on.
It knew too much about the past.

The houses I passed were silent, their doors still faded
by the sun. I could have knocked on any one
and said how the town was receding, how the air
had changed.

I'd recognise no one.

The car knew the tune I was singing. The trees
kept me in shade. I could tell the water
was in shadow. I knew enough not to look
while everything was still ahead of me.

BOY WITH ANIMAL

At least I can recognise the different
voices of the birds. I have learned at least
to distinguish. Today I will go outside,

the sky will be different to yesterday —
though I will take the same route and pass
the same people, their faces will be

yesterday's faces. I call up my today
face and it comes running towards me
like my own happy dog. People have

forgotten how to summon their animals.
I live on low land, with no immediate
height about me but the distance

is brilliantly vertical. It rises upwards
and keeps me safe. Whole afternoons
with my back to part of the world. I know

my animal, can see it clearly, even when
not pressed close, even now as I make
my way with no thoughts of returning.

TWO FIGURES

I saw them in the distance, always a little side by side,
talking a little to each other. On the quays
they stopped by the water, all scattered streetlight
and moon. All day I had the feeling of the window
at my back. I left to be outside, and walked
in the same direction towards the hill. They began
to climb its belly. Only halfway up I could tell
they were winded. I stopped by the church
with its own burial ground. I didn't know the order.
Through the wrought iron gate I could see
it was grassy between the stones. At the top of the hill
they circled back towards the barracks, and again
towards the town. I did the same. On the bridge
an icy wind blew up off the river, pushing them
nearer. I could hear the wind whipping their voices
out of shape. Close as could be, one or two
small words. I was sure, this time, I'd remember.

BRIDGE I

From a central point I could see the streets
were set at right angles to each other and ran
parallel with the river. Everything conformed
with the water's contours, which is to say
with the valley's. From undefined points
I could make out the turn that would take me
as far as the bridge. This was the appeal
as well as the point. I'd read the visitor
reports, how, on the whole, things disappoint.
The impression produced on the stranger is in no way…
The impression produced was of water flooding
the mudflats at high tide, of a warm July,
of a place where I was most… It was clear
how the town grew up, how it was put
in place. *The weather was the fairest we'd seen,*
no signs of… Though the town did
more and more begin to shape the lives
of those who felt less and less like themselves.
This was a little known fact. Most days
it wasn't perceptible. Even from the bridge,
which was supposedly where things converged,
I couldn't quite tell which of us was acting,
which of us was acting like ourselves.

THE BULLRING

I saw them again standing in a semi-circle
by the old bridge. I could hear words indicating
absence but didn't blame them as I too saw the town
in past tense. Someone asked about the blind gate.
It used to be… I turned my head. We were standing
on the former former where the dogs
pinned the bull's peppered snout. *A practice known as…*
Where was the bull? In this very place
or so very almost. The whole town
had an almostness to it. But the blind gate was further
back and the two were not related. I wanted to know
what the blind gate was for. I wanted a blind gate
for the bull, so his snout could be spared.
I almost asked, but someone mentioned the hangings.
That was later, difficult too to believe.
Nowadays we believe in demolition
and dual carriageways. Everyone laughed.
Nowadays, nowadays, nowadays.

BLIND GATES OF

Being a complete stranger I didn't see the gate.
In order to qualify a town must have four
of the following… Why was I imagining an orchard?
It must have been a memory of stolen apples.
On the medieval map I counted the number of gates —
certain ways in, certain ways out. There was no book
called *Blind Gates Of.* It was a given. The aerial
views were supposed to clarify but only obscured
the reassembling. My eyes were drawn to grey silos
filled with grain, or was it wood chip? Was this my first
skyline? On the eve of St. John there were several
monstrous bone fires. Being a complete stranger
I couldn't stand the stench. It was better to think
of apples lying full in the thick grass, red moons
circling red moons, apples circling apples.

BRIDGE II

It was further than I'd thought but I'd already left,
was already at the bridge somewhere near the end
of summer. I counted the arches, the steps between.
A bird's eye view. There were markings
I hadn't yet seen, the water going where I couldn't.
It was an urban scene, with places lying beyond.
This is to say there were perceptible boundaries,
something I learned standing astride a white line
in the middle of the road. *Here you can be in two places*
at the same time. I was here and here, there and there.
A house on either side, one that was mine,
one that was not. When I looked up, the surface
was mountain and the sound was the river splitting
the arches. The hollow was all town. I'd wanted
to see this for myself. In the centre the square —
more symmetry than geometry — still gave a sense
of enclosure. People still gathered, not so much
by design and never to see something burning.
It was more of a charm offensive, and it was beautiful.
Despite or in spite of? I was never really sure.

RIVER EDGE

And what is it about fish
swimming under the thin scum of the wash
forming and reforming its pattern in the sun.

What is it that makes the derelict
emerge so easily from the dark mouth of the station,
from the bridge where the trains run

in concurrent sentences from light to dark.
People throw objects over the green railings.
How many times do they have to fall

before they break the pattern of the water
where the fish swim in a continuous puddle
of discarded things. Reflected flags

fly high over the heads of the fish
whose bellies are so close to the ground.
Who knows anything about them?

For a while someone will come and scrape
the surface, someone will say they swam upstream
to be here, and there is still enough

of the filmy dark
to make of ourselves what we will.

WRECKAGE I

After I waded out I could see again the fullness
of the sky. Until then my view had been confined
to diminished diameters of blue. Was I bothered
by loneliness? A question I remembered, first.
Not with Stadtpark and the old museums,
but the question troubled me. On shore
I noticed the distinct smell of gas, or whatever
compound had been added to keep us safe.
It felt like the front of my house had been blown
out. With nothing to obstruct my view I peered
onto the street. I wanted to ask what had happened
and hurried towards the Ringstraße. It was easy
to follow the curve of the trams. Parts of the old
city slipped in and out of view. In the Volksgarten
I was frightened by the rose bushes. Bound
in their rough winter sacks, they looked like the last
species on earth, maimed and cowering
with nowhere left to go. There was drilling
on the streets, my ears ached. At Ruprechtskirche
I waited for the ringing to subside. But the city
was starting over, I was already too late.

an ordinary wind ran through the tall buildings.
The river was low, I had to lean on the railings
just to make it appear. Some crows bathed,
though it was nothing to fuss about.
News of floods and contamination filtered
through. *When we can't even drink the water…*
People took photographs, convinced they could see
a slick on the surface. It was impossible to tell
just by looking. So much depends upon distance
and estimations of far-off points. I was in
the vicinity but already running towards another.
It was better to look up where I couldn't see
what was left or right, only lights
that looked like the lights of reachable places.
Did yesterday resemble a specific place?
Did the river really heave itself up? Was it really
to blame for the way things turned out?

won't always look like this. Cicadas
in the planted trees won't always sing.
But there are other sounds to count on.
Ich Ich Ich — Ich kann nur im Präsens sprechen.
I lower the blinds to hide from the landscape,
on the opposite wall the one word I know
is crossed out. I present-tense speak,
mispronouncing words as recurrence.
I remember all the ways of saying today.
I remember today. There must be different
ways of arranging dates, different ways
of counting. How far can I go back
to this or that time? How much distance
does it take to forget? How many ways
to circumvent? The sound of the cicadas
is, for now, ever present, just as the sun
between high buildings is up for anyone.

LANDSCAPE WITH WINDOW

As the season changed it was harder to trust
the patterns of the landscape, the light
from the window, altered and altering.
The sky at a certain point could
correspond to summer, not dawn
but some August hour that looked
convincing. I had to accept the sea
merging with the sky, the view
becoming indistinct. What was outside
was outside, however it appeared.
I too was gaining distance, impartial
to the sun going on behind the clouds.
And it was going on, like everything
unseen, the strand visible
then obscured. For a while
things happened in a particular way,
in a particular place. On any street
it would have been the same. The low
lights made it difficult to see, a sort of
caution was required, which is true
of any seeing. Sometimes I could see
very far, other times, no further
than my window.

FIRST PART OF THE NIGHT

Days were plain sailing. Sun up, sun down,
moon over the… I was beginning to recognise
time. Turning the calendar every evening,
lifting the blinds at night so I could lower them
in the morning. It was already past June
when I began living in opposites.
Not wanting to appear idle, I began
to walk with purpose. Noticing some
repetitions — the flower stand
at the gates of the park, how flowers
must always have been sold there.
The same woman with her dog
and a very particular phrase, what was it
she was trying to tell him?
I passed the old river, and the carp,
followed them as far as the canal.
There were boats setting out — they had to
start from somewhere. The way things
in chronological order must start
at the beginning, something I was
beginning to understand.

BY BLUE AND YELLOW

I was walking the old street, remarking the buildings
that had stood, that were still standing. By the blue
and yellow hoarding there were small offerings
at what had once been the base of a door.
The cobbled street must have held some meaning,
must have been the point where it all began.
In some ways it was easy to tell the old
from the new, but sometimes I was never really sure.
I once thought the flickering lights were coded,
that some message was meant to reach through.
The lights being only a cover for the real
point of it all. Now it's the stone that confuses.
I counted the first three steps where the leaves
blew in, and the brass plates with the names
of my neighbours, who had always lived there.
The stairwell before me, my hand
on the railing. I could hear the cicadas
singing. Higher up could see clouds, then stars.

II

TRIPTYCH OF BIRTH YEARS FOR THE ARTIST NANO REID: 1905

Year of my birth of the waning moon crescent
on my skin in the month of March this is where
the joint pain will grow the records have begun
they are making a history of weather the sun
on the day of my birth was not captured the rain
fell in a sort of slant before it hit the pavement
and drew us in I must have been looking
in some direction I must have been drawn
to some corner of the room my eye fell upon

THEN I WENT DOWN THERE AND SUDDENLY BEGAN

to see things, the starlings on the wire, the islands
reappearing at low tide. The sea wasn't any sort
of blue, it had its own accord and could not
be replaced. The picture of the landscape
was not one I remembered. I used to think
there was nothing in it, had registered the outline,
not the detail. Now the detail was taking over
until the whole place had the look of somewhere
I'd known all along — the dab of white paint
on the stone put there to mark the highest tide.
To say this has been the warmest June on record
is to say it's the warmest I remember. I note
how I note the weather, remark ends and beginnings.
Like I'm supposed to? Like I'm supposed to.
This marks the end, I say, for the sake of the end.
I've read the journals of earlier lives. It wasn't
for the sake of the high tide that the wall
was marked. It had a meaning lost to me now.
Still, I'm glad to finally be here.

EVEN THE SKY

At night the land changes, so much dead air
descends. How long had I been counting steeples
from the walls of the old fort?
There was no one about. From here I could point
to houses I once lived in, buildings I remembered
that were no longer there. Easy to register
absence when there's so much evidence,
so much flat land. An entire forest
stacked on rows and rows of train carriages.
I once saw my house from a plane, was certain
I could see someone I knew at the door.
From a height you can tell what things
really are, can clearly proclaim the such and such
of anywhere. *Do you see it?* I would ask,
adjusting my eyes to be sure. But when
have I ever seen even the fullness
of the moon? Always the frustrating glare
at its edges. What would it look like
if it didn't look like this? A town's cut-out shape
in the night, where even the sky has a line
running through it.

LANDSCAPE WITH PARK

Sitting by the open window I could tell it was early
spring. And in the park there was no real reason
to doubt it. The river was supposed to be blue,
it took me three months to get there and even then
it was northern grey. But I was happy
as I floated past buildings that could have stood
for anything. At night I avoided certain areas, never
walked as far as Heumarkt, because of the Stadtpark,
because you never know. And when the blossoms
finally came out in a tangible way, I was afraid
to go in there in case the weather was wrong.
But I survived the winter and the weather
did change from day to day, and the sun
did sometimes make the morning worth it.

LANDSCAPE WITH ECLIPSE

I remember that fall into darkness
where you said the earth appeared
dead. And then I saw the sky
without any trace of blood in it
and thought a river can sometimes
have the sky in it but the sky
can more easily absorb all the colours
of the earth until it's thick as earth
and will not move.
I too felt the plunge
but from a window and not the top
of a hill. I thought of you then
when I peered out. I was seeing you
as you noted the year
it would happen again, and now
that year had arrived. *Hello*, I said
but there was no reply, only dull
roofs on a darkening street.
When I think of it now it was just
like you said — shadow falling,
and yes, then we fell.

LANDSCAPE WITH FALLING SUITCASE

I saw the night rise above the city, I saw the dome
as it once appeared in a dream. Why did my eye
always catch it? It was an ordinary thing to do,
to look up. In the month of February there was
space to move about the streets, more ways
to walk than I remembered, more ways to arrive
at the centre. I found the mix of past and present
slightly distressing. As I turned a corner the smell
became a stench. The sky was watery red, the stone
a bluish blue. I could not make the almond tree
blossom for the sake of something beautiful.
For the sake of the sky someone said
they'd remain here. This sky isn't every sky
despite the way the world is mapped out.
If it wasn't so beautiful it would be easier
to forget. The effect of the light is what really
bothers. All of the trouble came from commencing,
how unfamiliar the whole concept of town or village
must have been. To be born and grow up in.
Was born and grew up in... Why did the dome
come crashing down in the dream? The meaning
is wholly subjective, it's related to the dreamer's
mind, that is to say their state of well-being,
which is often a greyish-grey in the process
of becoming a true match for the sky. In the story
it was a suitcase that came crashing down, no bones
were broken, which is not to say no one was hurt.
Someone is always injured, or soon to be injured,
even if the story would have us believe otherwise.

OF THE DARK

Not the sun but its reflection, slow beam
from behind the trees, and on the water
a channel of light stilled the sea

on either side. How the landscape changes.
Was the light there real, or just my perception
of it? Was this only part of the night? Sounds

made everything uncertain, until something
created a shiver, though I knew it was nonsense
to shiver just because of the dark.

But the proportions had changed, everything
seemed like it could be something else, and it was
something else. Slow harbinger don't appear —

I don't want to know. I refuse to take your life
into mine, even if your wings beat just out of sight.
You look unreal but are made of real things.

In the morning you won't be the same,
or at least I won't think you the same.

LANDSCAPE WITH BRONZE LIONS

I went looking for the two bronze lions.
I knew the place, thought it could be reached
from anywhere. It was a matter of setting out
or going back. So many landscapes to revisit,
all from a book I'd read — *Today is an impossible*
word for me. Today is also an impossible place.
The light cycle of the traffic, how much can I
remember in two minutes? How much can I change?
I'm crossing from the Fourth to the Third District,
how much of this would I know if the numbers
weren't directional? Yesterday I came the same way.
I can lift landscape from anywhere, can make it
mean nothing to me, withdraw my affection
like someone carrying on from *used* to *be*.

SECOND PART OF THE NIGHT

I was fully familiar with the street,
knew to be careful in traffic. I was
supposed to obtain abundant sleep
but the noise made me remember
where I was. Always a car passing,
always en route to somewhere.
No crime, just the usual things —
someone crossing the street
trying to reach someone who is
somewhere else. It wasn't as if
they were knocking on my door,
even if I have the same address
as ten other people and two
fictional characters. But at night
someone did come to photograph
the building next door. Small
embellishments were required
to hold the place together.
There was nothing special
about this — all the streets were
crumbling. I had to learn
to think in gains, to love how
from my window I could see part
of the sky. And not by a hair's
breadth or the skin of my teeth —
I would not think in *barelys*.
Our windows are dark. People go
to bed early or go without
light. Low voices on the thin air,
an entire street monologuing.
Is that what I'm hearing?

SOLAR OR LUNAR

it made no difference. I could find my way
even when the lights went out and the dog
stood in place. The sea coming in was easy
to recognise, the optics straightforward,
unlike the eye faced with the sun. Things
appeared closer than they were, the shock
of moon on the horizon, a voice
on the stairwell, ascending or descending.
Summer ended, or the time of summer,
so the calendar said, a word I could never
get right. I sat in the sun. It wasn't the same.
The hour wasn't tomorrow's, it was time
falling back, though no one was in danger.
There were parts of the day I failed
to recognise, like someone unpractised,
happy for the distance I'd gained,
knowing the hours were unequal, how one
could be sunk and sunk under. How easy
it was to change.

LANDSCAPE WITH CURVE

I marked all the passages pertaining to time,
traced and retraced the hours in the day,
the angle of the sun when the light fell
on the curve of the street. Was this
the exact place? Was I seeing it again
for the first time? It was late in the day
when I came upon the boarded-up building,
the old name still visible, though it wasn't
an exact match — could one small word
really make a difference. Was it vital?
I knew it wasn't made up, but what was
related to what? The trouble of tracing
one voice over and over again. Why did
the names have to match? Pointless to
come the same way for fear of change.
If I really looked I'd see it was unreal.
No one was walking from one house
to another, no one was crossing the street.
The sound of the telephone was now
the sound of my alarm. I had to keep
changing the tone so when the sun lit
the stone it wouldn't be the first
sound of the day. It wouldn't be a vanishing
to round the curve and no longer be able
to see back. It would simply be a point
from which to look at things
like they weren't disappearing.

WRECKAGE II

After I waded out the sea turned its back on me. It's true
I was lonesome having been so swallowed up.
I expected a cold tinge to the air but the night was full
of warmth, of something already seen. I wasn't sure
in which direction the centre lay, would have known
had I been here before. Few lights in the houses, strange
to see into people's homes like this. A girl on her bed
with a soft toy as a pillow. I should have signalled
to draw the blinds but hurried on. I was in the ruins
of a city. The streets had a peculiar smell, it wasn't
dust but was akin to crumbling. White powder
at the base of the buildings as if someone had tried
to burn away the snow. The outsides daubed
with plaster but the smell seeped through. People
were doing their best to cover it up. I began
to smell it on my clothes. It burrowed in
the way bad dreams burrow into the day.
Lone walkers with their dogs trailing behind,
not much else to see. I returned to the shore,
waited for the tide to reach the rocks.
Whatever had happened it was time to go back.

LÉGENDE

The remains of the ship can be seen
only at low tide. Could a swimmer cut their feet
on the hull's bones if they were to come down
hard from a wave? There's the wave,
then there's the thing that's covered
by the wave. This is what we stare into —
salt stings, blood droplets dissolve into foam.
In July everyone leaves. And I still don't
know if it was the people or the place
I couldn't stand. I was warned not to listen
but it was only a matter of time
before I was cupping my hand to my ear
to see if the sound was real. I looked again
and could make out the whole of the hull
beneath, then a face and then a face.
I knew then it comes quickly, or not at all.

NO HUMAN FIGURES

It could have been any city, could have been
any time, except for the constant impression
the day made. I must think in time
so as not to waste it. How many years have I spoiled
by disobeying the calendar? Useless to think
time is made up, but how to account for lost hours?
In the Englisher Garten a woman asked us
to step aside so she could photograph the river
without intrusion — no human figures
except the one she remembered,
bathing his feet when the heat ceased
to be bearable. I wonder what time it was
when he stepped into the water. I must forget
her face — I won't add another to memory.
It must have been August because our dog
was still alive, but I refuse to remember
if the leaves were already beginning to fall.

LANDSCAPE WITH SINGLE LINE

And I should remember more but the scenes
drift, the clock reads 1 a.m. even though
it is eight in the morning. The sun pierces me
in the eye, the sky is pink and sometimes
there is fog. It is in the fog that I can see
the branches of the tree most clearly.
And sometimes there is rain and the rattle
of the magpie, when I am most vulnerable.
It was a German town, something about
having little to do. There have to be places
I doubt I'll ever see. Some things
have to be spared, like where the town comes
to an end — I say where the town comes
to an end but have no clear vision of its ending.
Some things must be spared where I am most...
Of all the things I've read I think instead
of the little I've retained — *it pierces me*
in the eye, where I am most vulnerable to beauty.

LANDSCAPE WITH QUESTION

When the question comes again I see
only hollow landscapes lapsing into sun
as if time were space and not just the absence
of a plausible answer, a sense equation that anyone
could recognise as a sensible way of structuring
thought. And it was always there, sure to be one
of one. But how best to signal miscomprehension?
I shrug my shoulders or move my hands
in some sort of gesturing gesture but in the end
I must admit it is not of my grasping. The sequence
is sun into moonlight, an object closing in on itself,
a city where I once walked, or the river rising and falling.
At the crowded intersection titled *People in the City*
I was part of the arrangement. One foot before
the other, one thought into another but no one
lapsing into an image of rotting fruit. It must never
be like that — to the question that is not even fair
to the asker, I make no fair reply.

III

TRIPTYCH OF BIRTH YEARS FOR THE ARTIST NANO REID: 1910

I was my daughter was my son was my granddaughter
was my grandson was my sister was my brother was
my mother was on this day born in this year when
the weather was all around us and my sister thought
I was born just for her holding me proud and tight
like a task she could achieve on a bright day the sun
shone and the rain for once stood off not that it
would have made a difference not one I ever could
remember the room was positioned one way and I
another and outside that room was another and
another still where someone said they didn't blame
the child for crying where someone said that must be
the new child and how the sun at least shone and it's
nice at least that it's not like when someone is buried
and we all must hope for rain

MAY OR SEPTEMBER

I may have remarked the first day of summer, may
have noted the moon take on the sun's colour. The light
gave the same impression. I knew the distance
was a city, that the flickering lights were only an effect —
rogue debris of distortion. No semblance orbiting,
just the outlines re-establishing themselves, the roots
of the city growing down. You can miss a place
you've disliked. A room or a station. No hard feelings —
just the slight tether of a thread, like the cord of a blind
going up on May or September. May or September?
I was walking the old street with the blue and yellow
buildings. The lights hanging low, with no intention
to embellish. I did discover something there though,
did find a particular place. The sky was sudden
between the clouds and a few blunt stars
were all I could see. No flicker to flicker out.

WHEN THE BUTCHER

When the butcher comes to your door
it can only mean one thing. The dead
don't need food and the living can't swallow
a morsel, but suddenly food everywhere.
Do you remember the butcher's tears?
He didn't have a free hand to hide them.
How had I forgotten the trays of tea
and coffee? And how long had I been
drinking from a cup that wasn't mine?
Small white cup with a deep blue trim
that made me think of the sea, always
there since before I could remember
a time in which there was no need
to remember, in which I knew exactly
how time played out from here to here to here
and all the blah blah blah of it, until suddenly
the butcher is standing at your door
and there's no two ways about it.

LANDSCAPE WITH CROWS

I saw how the present conformed to its past,
rising as it did from what remained.
There were things under things and things
inside things. This was the first thing
I noticed. Then the birds that flew in
and startled. Except they had more claim
than I, standing in the draft as I was.
Dead sister? Lost friend? It was the wrong
time to ask, or the wrong sort of question.
The light through the lightbox moved so brilliantly
it appeared as a hoax. This wasn't the case.
It was previously recorded as prehistory.
This is how we imagine it to be. I imagine
the walls as I once saw them, the scenes
and pictures I'd conjured up as explanation.
Dull objects that someone has to gather
in order to know. The birds and I
among the evidence. All that time ago.

BLADES

Next time I neared the centre, the grass
was high. Had it not just been shorn?
I usually took the circular path
but the blades towered above me.
At the entrance to the sewer, people
adjusted lights on their hats
so they could make their way down.
It wasn't a real event, no one was
hiding. It was only approximation.
The first time I heard the crow
at my window I assumed it was
a bad omen. It must have been here
that I was at my most pathetic —
another creature's life a message
to my own? You can live anywhere
for two years, but what happens then?
I don't want to leave the banks of the…
I don't want to move when the light
changes. I must recycle this walk
or wait to see them emerge. Will they
have something of the sunken
about them? Or will it be like now
when I hear a crow
I think nothing but crow.

SPELL OF THE WOOD

The dream of the tree looks the same
at the beginning as it will at the end.

Insects burrow the dark, dream
in the soil. The dream reaches the roots

of the tree that is not burning.
The tree is not dreaming in the way

the insects dream, or the other animals
that are dreaming in the forest.

Shelter is not the same as hiding,
fire not the same as burning.

The tree's dream can often be disturbed
by an axe, or a knife

carving a human name.
The tree notes the knife

as it notes the insect bite
at the edge of a leaf.

But the tree cannot be
expelled from its dream

the way people are.
The dream of the tree

is a dream of any season,
of any forest, of any flame.

A FIRE IN THE OPEN

Light obeys the sky. Weather dresses me. Beautiful sunsets
seen through flame.

Where is the furnace and what are they burning?

It's hard to calculate the distance,
though it can't be far. The air polishes a flame
until it snaps and bristles. But the sky

is beautiful. The sky is a treat.
We are pillars holding up the city. The season wills it.

We warm ourselves on a summer night. Empty hands
above flames, the sound of animals moving
in a nearby field, the sound of people leaving.

Someone is breaking sticks, snapping their thin spines.

The fire throws parts of us into light, tiny craters
form in the fabric of our clothes.

If ever the earth were to end
it would surely look something like this.

If ever the earth were to end we would surely look.

But the sky is beautiful, the sky is a treat.
Whatever will burn is burning.

CANAL AND RIVER

Is it the burning bull at the centre or the sun
I remember? Canal and river, a fisherman
in waders, a boy passing under.

At spring tide the boy moved through the valley
passing red and blue fields, passing
parallel waters.

Was it still summer or already autumn?

Partial month of leaves partially green. A boy
in water, alive for part of the day, in this aspect
of the season.

River right, river left.

I watch the current, the fisherman in waders
who I always thought had dragged him out.

Could the boy graze your leg the way river weed
skims the skin when you push off from the jetty?

I push off from the jetty —
I know the weed can't harm me.

The sun is high, the water is dark water.

LANDSCAPE WITH FACTORY

You can see a lot from the hill, the grey breath
of the factory, its red lights, always on.
And other hills beyond this one, where the earth
is also red. I remember flying over a blue
lake. It could have been the last thing I saw
or the image I returned to after something else
occurred. The water in the lake
behaves in a similar way, it warms in summer
while its layers grow cool, no hidden currents
just the wind in the clear.
It has a cold mind, like the mind flying over —
empty of earthly things. I know the smoke
makes it difficult to breathe, in small ways
I don't yet recognise. In summer the leaves
hide much of the grey. Small particles
are still borne on the air. I'm ashamed of this
but tell no one — I can hold my breath
when it matters most.

LANDSCAPE WITH SLEEPING DOG

The street appeared as I first and last
saw it, in March light, in December sun.
I knew the moon was in winter. Was I
there too? The dog barking in his sleep
may have confirmed it, but how much
did he know that he was barking?
The muscles of his legs approximated
the real way he was moving in the world
he'd slipped into. Sometimes it was
the street or the road leading to the sea.
Waves over the dome, the horizon sucking
the colour from a sky where dream
equals city equals dream equals city.
Though it wasn't the same it was still
the same place. Like I was and wasn't
the same when I leaned from the viewing
point down to where I'd just been.
I'd walked all day without seeing a single
tree, which barely merits mention.
Before, I might suffer from expecting
to see what was no longer there, like leaves
imprinting on the concrete. I've learnt
to adapt, to make suitable things
for new purpose.

ERRIGAL

The picture kept returning, like the real colour
of the sky at night. I recounted the contours,
moving back and forth across the city.
Did this recall anything? I recalled coming
down the wrong side of the mountain
in the June heat. I recalled the river in September
holding more colour than it was used to.
It wasn't the buildings against a backdrop
of blue that I missed but I did miss something.
Something that was somewhere and still going
on. Most things go on as before, which makes it
easier to believe that we are looking at a faithful
copy of the actual scene. *I must recount*,
someone said, then recounted. The scene
is as the picture would have it appear.
It was hard to know whether the calendar
had any influence — a before or after,
or some other quality. Streets, churches
cathedrals, mountains, and the high grass
all woven to a facsimile that converged here.
I recognised it as the place where I was from.
Oh was it any sort of place to be? The Middle Ages
were resplendent by comparison. You could go
outside to where no one had been, places
that had not yet been replicated. A view
of the region surrounded any observer, even if
they didn't wish to look. From such definable
characteristics it wasn't possible to turn away.
It would hurt more to avert your eyes,
even with the hint of a boundary forming.

where part of the night is still day,
you don't realise you're above
ground until everything beneath is light.
What was your life like back then?
Greyer and greyer, the sky deteriorated
the further I ascended, as if
there were two skies, one having
nothing to do with the other.
Were you practicing your grief?
I was practising as best I could.
Greyer and greyer. I was
deteriorating, the way over time
the story always changes.
In July I can say, *this time last year* —
but there's part of me
that can never really be in July,
where no one can stand it.
Greyer and greyer, another part
of the sky was deteriorating,
the first part of the night
was practising. There were two
skies. Above ground I can say,
this time last year you were
practising July. Your life
back then. Greyer and greyer,
though part of the night
was still day.

LANDSCAPE WITH LIGHTS

Three stars to set your watch by.
That's how we know. The sun has set.

Are we white to red or green to blue? Are we radiating
from the centre? Let's wave. Let's accumulate.

The darkest part of the map is in water but even the sea
can light up like an inverse planetarium.

If something were to fall it would fall upwards
and we'd all run out instead of in. We'd welcome it off.
No one could mistake it for a ship or a tree, no misreading

of the clouds, or the shape of the clouds.

It would happen in the darkest part of the night.

Everyone would see it, everyone would know
how below the light there were humans waving.

LANDSCAPE WITH SPRIG OF HOLLY

All those markers falling in on themselves —
yellow streetlight, a mountain
under a clear moon, some deer in the snow.
Working backwards from a close-up
sprig of holly I settled on July, etched
a make-do circle that was sure
to commemorate something. If not
yet falling leaves then at least some slow
change in the life of the tree,
or the nightly pattern
of the stars — they are not nothing,
even though I know only ugly ways
to say so. Or the clock set
to see a blood moon
sink in the sky. Arrival
then departure. The day
we followed the river, the day
the river disappeared. Someone
out howling at the moon, or just
someone howling. The circle
of my pen to remind me
how I must above all else
discriminate my days.

LANDSCAPE WITH TREES

The time of year was visible
in the afternoon sky,
but I was still thinking in numbers.

It was the second month of a year
that had not yet said, *this year*
will be this or that.

By the twelfth we would know,
but we were still
in the darkest season, in the grey light.

The memory of a tree ablaze
was a memory of a tree ablaze
in a concrete park, on the borders
of a town.

Who set the tree to burning?

Someone who wouldn't hear of the falling
leaves, someone who said, *winter*
won't put this out.

In the grey light the trees I could see
looked the same. We were at the limits
of the season, and the sky

couldn't be mistaken
for a blaze — its vague light only a kind
of reaching through.

LANDSCAPE WITH CHANGE OF TENSE

I was still in the old hour when the sun
took its usual route. Did the hour really
make a difference if I recognised the day?

If only I could teach myself time or learn
to displace it, without moving forward or back.

Certain details must be verified. Things I could
have said or withheld, the line of my own thought
disappearing like a key between the boards, or

the landscape of the window slowly becoming
another country. The sun wasn't inventing

but it had to catch up. The names had to keep
changing. It was only when the river appeared
that I knew where I was. Something had

occurred or had at least stopped occurring,
now it was something else, a glass of water
becoming a glass.

But it wasn't really like that. Even if it was
helpful, it was no way to think about the past,
where I must have set one day apart

from another, must have said, *that was today*,
and it was.

NOTES

Some of the poems take their title or partial title from the paintings of the Irish Modernist artist Nano Reid, and, in places, include quotes from Reid. A number of poems in the book incorporate quotes or partial quotes from Ingeborg Bachmann's *Malina*, translated by Philip Boehm (Penguin, 1990), as well as visitor reports and articles adapted from James Garry's *The Streets and Lanes of Drogheda* (Old Drogheda Society, 1999) and Cornelius Kelly's *The Grand Tour of Limerick* (Cailleach Books, 2004). These, and other borrowings, I have listed below. For all unconscious borrowings I am equally accountable and equally grateful.

TRIPTYCH OF BIRTH YEARS FOR THE ARTIST NANO REID — The Irish Modernist artist Nano Reid was born on March 1, 1900, but throughout her lifetime often gave her date of birth as 1905 or 1910. In approaching Reid's work over the course of this collection, I decided to accept all three given dates.

LANDSCAPE WITH DAFFODILS — 'Sometimes I still get a little anxious when I notice the first magnolia blossoms, but you can't always make a fuss about that.'; 'Just stay calm, think about the Stadtpark, think about the leaf, think about the garden in Vienna'. Ingeborg Bachmann, *Malina*, tr. Philip Boehm.

The broad arrow at Meadow View, Drogheda, Co. Louth is 140ft, marking the highest point above sea level in Drogheda.

WATER IN SHADOW — Takes its title from Nano Reid's painting *Water in Shadow*, exhibited as part of 'Nano Reid ADAMANTINE', Highlanes Gallery, Drogheda, October 2021 to January 2022.

BOY WITH ANIMAL — Takes its title from Nano Reid's watercolour *Boy with Animal.* The painting was exhibited as part of the 'Nano Reid Retrospective', Municipal Gallery, Dublin, and Ulster Museum, Belfast, November 1974 to February 1975, catalogue no. 77.

BLIND GATES OF — 'It is difficult to believe nowadays that four persons were hanged on the scaffold which stood at the bottom of Peter Street, just opposite the Tholsel'; 'Unluckily it happened to be the Eve of St. John — a great Roman Catholic holiday, and at our return to our Inn we were forced to pass by several monstrous bone fires (actually made of bones) [...] and by the time we got to our Inn, the whole air was impregnated with the vile stench.' James Garry, *The Streets and Lanes of Drogheda.*

RIVER EDGE — Takes its title from Nano Reid's painting *River Edge*, exhibited as part of 'Nano Reid ADAMANTINE', Highlanes Gallery, Drogheda, October 2021 to January 2022.

The railings of the Zollamtssteg, a pedestrian bridge across the River Wien in Vienna are green. Directly underneath the Zollamtssteg is the Zollamtsbrücke [Customs Office Bridge], where the U4 metro line has operated since 1978.

WRECKAGE I — Takes its title from Nano Reid's painting *Wreckage No. 1*, exhibited as part of 'Nano Reid ADAMANTINE', Highlanes Gallery, Drogheda, October 2021 to January 2022.

'No, I was not lonely. There were museums, galleries, the walks in the *Stadtpark*, visiting the old churches.' H. D., *Tribute to Freud.*

FIRST PART OF THE NIGHT — 'The second part of the night doesn't have anything to do with the first, two different nights are housed in one night'. Ingeborg Bachmann, *Malina*, tr. Philip Boehm.

LANDSCAPE WITH PARK — 'Out of consideration I turn at the Heumarkt, threatened by the proximity of the Stadtpark, by its shadows and dark figures, [...] Because of the Stadtpark, you never know'. Ingeborg Bachmann, *Malina*, tr. Philip Boehm.

LANDSCAPE WITH ECLIPSE — 'We had fallen. It was extinct. There was no colour. The earth was dead.' Virginia Woolf, diary entry for June 30, 1927, in *A Writer's Diary.*

LANDSCAPE WITH FALLING SUITCASE — 'one realises how foreign the whole concept either of town or village must be to the Irish'. Geoffrey Grigson, quoted in Cornelius Kelly (ed.), *The Grand Tour of Limerick* (Cailleach Books, 2004).

LANDSCAPE WITH BRONZE LIONS — Ungargasse 9 is in Vienna's Third District. This is Ivan's address in *Malina.*

SECOND PART OF THE NIGHT — '"With a little more courage you will be able to master upcoming difficulties. Be careful in traffic. Obtain abundant sleep."'; 'In the first night it's still the day, [...] You don't realise it's really night until the second night comes'. Ingeborg Bachmann, *Malina*, tr. Philip Boehm.

LÉGENDE — Takes its title from Nano Reid's painting *Légende*, exhibited as part of 'Nano Reid ADAMANTINE', Highlanes Gallery, Drogheda, October 2021 to January 2022. Though Reid references another shipwreck located on Mornington Strand in Co. Meath, Ireland, the shipwreck I have in mind is the 'Eilean Glas', stranded on Mornington Strand on May 1, 1980.

'Things come quickly or not at all.' Nano Reid, quoted in 'Nano Reid: Harriet Cooke talks to the painter', *The Irish Times*, July 6, 1973.

'I was a year in London altogether, and I was never more miserable in my life. I hated and loathed it. I don't know if it was the place or the people'. Nano Reid, Interview with Marion FitzGerald, *The Irish Times*, October 2, 1965.

LANDSCAPE WITH SINGLE LINE — The single line in italics is borrowed from Ingeborg Bachmann's poem 'Autumn Maneuver', *Darkness Spoken: The Collected Poems*, tr. Peter Filkins.

LANDSCAPE WITH CROWS — 'There were things under things, as well as things inside things.'; 'dead brother? lost friend?' H. D., *Tribute to Freud*.

SPELL OF THE WOOD — This poem was written for the Kurdish poet Ilhan Sami Çomak, as part of PEN Norway's 'Free the Poet' campaign, organised by Caroline Stockford. Çomak was released on November 26, 2024, following thirty-years in solitary confinement in a Turkish prison. The poem takes its title from Nano Reid's painting *Spell of the Wood*, exhibited as part of 'Nano Reid ADAMANTINE', Highlanes Gallery, Drogheda, October 2021 to January 2022. When writing this poem, and thinking about Çomak's case, I took inspiration from 'The Time of the Lime Trees', a short section in

Olga Tokarczuk's *Primeval and Other Times*, tr. Antonia Lloyd-Jones. The poem is also in memory of Breda Wall Ryan.

A FIRE IN THE OPEN — Takes its title from Nano Reid's painting *A Fire in the Open*, exhibited as part of 'Nano Reid ADAMANTINE', Highlanes Gallery, Drogheda, October 2021 to January 2022.

CANAL AND RIVER —Takes its title from Nano Reid's painting *Canal and River in Autumn*, exhibited at the Venice Biennale in 1950. It is part of the collection of the National Gallery of Ireland. The banks of the Alte Donau [Old Danube] river in Vienna are lined with public bathing jetties.

LANDSCAPE WITH SLEEPING DOG — 'How much does he know that he is barking.' Gertrude Stein, *The Geographical History of America or the Relation of Human Nature to the Human Mind.*

ERRIGAL —Takes its title from Mount Errigal in Donegal. It was also the name of Nano Reid's house in Drogheda.

ALTERNATIVE VERSION OF THE NIGHT — 'Malina: What was your life like back then? Me: At three in the morning my face would turn grayer and grayer, I slowly deteriorated'. Ingeborg Bachmann, *Malina*, tr. Philip Boehm.

The line 'I was practising my grief' is borrowed from 'Ghostwriter', Act One of Episode 757 of the *This American Life* podcast, titled 'The Ghost in the Machine'.

ACKNOWLEDGEMENTS

Thanks are due to the editors of the following publications in which some of these poems, or versions of them, first appeared: *Banshee*, *Cyphers*, *Hold Open the Door: A Commemorative Anthology from the Ireland Chair of Poetry* (UCD Press, 2020), *Poetry Ireland Review*, *PN Review*, *Poetry Wales*, *Stand*, *The Irish Times*, *The Stinging Fly*, *Washing Windows V: Women Revolutionise Irish Poetry, 1975–2025* (Arlen Press, 2025), *Words That Walk Through Walls: World Poets Writing with Ilhan Sami Çomak* (Palewell Press, 2024).

My sincere gratitude to Michael Schmidt, John McAuliffe, and Andrew Latimer. My gratitude to Aoife Ruane and Stephen Hodgins at the Highlanes Gallery in Drogheda, for an invitation to speak on this book while it was a work in progress. Sincere gratitude to the historian Brendan Matthews for generously sharing his research and knowledge on Nano Reid and the history of the town of Drogheda. Brendan's walking tour of 'Nano Reid's Drogheda', provided in conjunction with the Highlanes Gallery during their 'Nano Reid: ADAMANTINE' exhibition in 2022, remains among the most insightful accounts of Reid's life and art I have encountered to date. It was integral in helping me to think about Reid's deep appreciation of the layered temporal spaces in the landscapes of Drogheda. I am also grateful to the authors, editors, and contributors of the following books, for guiding me: Nathan O'Donnell and Aoife Ruane (eds.), *Nano Reid: ADAMANTINE* (Highlanes Gallery, 2022); Ted Greene, *Drogheda: Its Place in Ireland's History* (Ted Greene, 2006); Declan Mallon, *Nano Reid* (Sunnyside, 1994); Helen M. Roe, *Monasterboice and its Monuments* (Dundalgan Press, 1993). The author gratefully acknowledges a Literature Bursary awarded by the Arts Council of Ireland in 2021. A portion of this manuscript was completed during a residency at the Heinrich Böll Cottage, Achill Island, in September 2025.

I am grateful to Sasha Dugdale for her friendship, and for sending me H. D.'s *Tribute to Freud.* I am grateful to Don Mee Choi for her friendship, and for recommending that I read Ingeborg Bachmann's *Malina*. I am grateful to Ellen Dillon, for her friendship in a new city.